Sunflowers

Contents

Getting started	page 2
Seeds	page 4
The seeds grow	page 6
Into the garden	page 8
The sunflowers grow	page 10
Higher and higher	page 12
Sunflower snacks	page 14
Glossary	page 16

Written by
Emma Lynch

Getting started

You need:
- thirty plastic flower pots
- thirty sunflower seeds
- some **compost**
- one roll of clingfilm.

In March, grow the seeds in the flower pots inside.
In early May, transfer the sunflowers to the garden.

Seeds

compost

seed

1 First, fill all thirty flower pots with compost. Pat the compost down firmly.
2 Now **sow** the sunflower seeds, one per pot.

3   Water the compost well.
4   Put some clingfilm on top of each flower pot.

The seeds grow

5   Keep the flower pots in a dry, sunny spot inside.
6   Water the compost.

In about thirteen days you will see a small **shoot**. The **roots** grow down and the shoots get bigger.

Into the garden

seedlings

7   Keep the flower pots inside until there is no winter frost.

8   In early spring, find a sunny spot in the garden.

The sunflowers grow

earth

9   Put the sunflowers in the earth.
10 Water the seedlings.

Protect the sunflowers from caterpillars, slugs, wind and cold.

Look out for caterpillars! They like to munch sunflowers.

Higher and higher

The sunflowers will flower all through the summer.

The sunflowers grow higher and higher, and further up into the sky!

How high did they grow?
Did they grow higher than you?

Sunflower snacks

Sunflower seeds make a tasty treat.

When the sunflowers die, shake out their seeds. Keep them in a bag.

birdfeeder

Birds like sunflower seeds, too. Tip some seeds into a bird feeder for the birds to eat in winter.

Glossary

compost   a mix of garden rubbish that is good for growing flowers

roots   the part of a flower that grows in the earth

shoot   the new or first part of a flower to grow

sow   put seeds in compost or earth